Core Skills in English

Assessment Activities and Answers

Book 1

Folens Publishers

Contents

Editor: Edward Rippeth Layout artist: Suzanne Ward

First published 1995 by Folens Limited, Albert House, Apex Business Centre, Boscombe Road, Dunstable, LU5 4RL, England.

ISBN 185276 655-7

Printed in Singapore by Craft Print

Introduction

English is at the centre of all learning. Pupils must develop an awareness of the essentials of grammar and spelling plus the skills of using language appropriately and competently if they are not to be disadvantaged in later life.

Core Skills in English is a series that aims to introduce pupils to the important features of the English language and to enable them to develop their ability to use and understand English. The series covers the essential skills of speaking, listening, reading and writing.

It concentrates on fundamental skills which are essential for effective, accurate and fluent communication.

The series develops pupils' ability to comprehend written passages and uses both grammar and comprehension in a series of relevant and structured exercises. Passages have been carefully chosen to provide a wide variety of interesting material from both literary and non-fiction texts.

How **Core Skills in English** works

- **Comprehension**
  Passages are of varying length and complexity. The pupil is asked a series of questions. In some cases the answers are explicit in the passage, while in others they are implicit. Some questions go beyond the confines of the passage and draw upon pupils' research skills. In addition there are a number of exercises that are designed specifically to encourage pupils to look for meaning in writing rather than merely to decode words.
  Comprehension passages lend themselves to a number of differing approaches. They can be used by an individual pupil or by groups of pupils, providing the basis for useful work on speaking and listening.

- **Grammar and Punctuation**
  Basic grammatical structures and key punctuation points are covered progressively throughout the series enabling pupils to build upon and consolidate skills.

- **Written style**
  Opportunities are offered for pupils to write in a variety of forms for a variety of purposes and audiences. In each book there are several sections that aim to broaden and develop pupils' style of writing. These vary from drawing attention to over-used words and suggesting alternatives to extending sentence construction. Pupils' vocabulary is broadened through a series of structured exercises.

Using this book

This Answer and Assessment Book gives teachers answers to the exercises in the textbook in order to save them time. It also provides a number of photocopiable activity and assessment sheets so that pupils' progress, knowledge and skills can be assessed more easily.

Pages 6 and 7

Jenny the Donkey

Questions

1. How were the ten pounds to be won?
   They could be won by anyone who could ride the vicious donkey twice round the ring.
2. Who liked to ride bareback?
   Big Tom Brown liked to ride bareback.
3. What terrified the donkey?
   The donkey was terrified of the noise of a bursting balloon.
4. What happened to Tom Brown at the start of his second round of the ring?
   Tom Brown was thrown by the scared donkey.
5. How was the clown dragged out of the ring?
   He was dragged out of the ring by the donkey.

The Full Stop

(A)

1. my friend has a bow and arrow
   My friend has a bow and arrow.
2. we saw a cowboy film
   We saw a cowboy film.
3. the chief smoked a peace-pipe
   The chief smoked a peace-pipe.
4. she lived with her husband in a large wigwam
   She lived with her husband in a large wigwam.
5. all the young braves danced around the campfire
   All the young braves danced around the campfire.
6. they traded their guns for buffalo hides
   They traded their guns for buffalo hides.
7. a pony galloped into the army fort
   A pony galloped into the army fort.
8. there was a young warrior behind the rock
   There was a young warrior behind the rock.
9. soon the witch doctor began praying for rain
   Soon the witch doctor began praying for rain.
10. the waggon-train was attacked
    The waggon-train was attacked.

Page 7 continued

(B)

1. mary called with her friend nora today i showed them my new pet rabbit
   Mary called with her friend Nora today. I showed them my new pet rabbit.
2. we had to stay inside all day i was delighted when the rain stopped
   We had to stay inside all day. I was delighted when the rain stopped.
3. the outlaws stopped the coach and robbed the passengers everybody was terrified
   The outlaws stopped the coach and robbed the passengers. Everybody was terrified.
4. the wolf called the frog and the bear they promised to help him
   The wolf called the frog and the bear. They promised to help him.
5. the shepherd watched over his flock the wolf did not dare come near
   The shepherd watched over his flock. The wolf did not dare come near.
6. the rocket lifted off it was going on a long voyage into outer space
   The rocket lifted off. It was going on a long voyage into outer space.
7. she worked long hours on the farm she had the finest herd of cattle in the land
   She worked long hours on the farm. She had the finest herd of cattle in the land.
8. a huge pirate stood on the deck his name was blackbeard
   A huge pirate stood on the deck. His name was Blackbeard.
9. snow fell during the night when i awoke, i wanted to make a snowman
   Snow fell during the night. When I awoke, I wanted to make a snowman.
10. the summer morning was bright and fair we set out for the seaside
    The summer morning was bright and fair. We set out for the seaside.

(C)

Long, long ago the Indians had no fire. The only fire in the world was kept by three ugly witches. They hated the Indian tribes. The witches took turns at guarding their precious fire and nobody could even get a spark from it.

Page 9

Snowy, the Polar Bear

Questions

1. In what part of the world does Snowy live?
   Snowy lives in the frozen lands of the Arctic.
2. Why is he called the "white hunter"?
   He is huge, white and an expert hunter.
3. How is it shown that the polar bear has great strength?
   He is so strong that a single blow from his paw could break the neck of an ox.
4. Why does he not freeze in the Arctic waters?
   Snowy's layers of fat stop him freezing in the Arctic waters.
5. What protection has he from the glare of the snow?
   Snowy has special eyelids that shield his eyes from the glare of the snow and ice.
6. Why does Snowy not slip on the ice?
   Snowy does not slip on the ice because the soles of his feet are padded with fur.
7. What is the bear's favourite food?
   Snowy's favourite food is seal flesh.
8. What enemies has the polar bear?
   The polar bear's enemies are the killer whale, the walrus and man.
9. Where are the cubs born?
   The cubs are born in a deep cave or snow tunnel.
10. How does the Inuit kill the polar bear?
    The Inuit waits by a breathing hole in the ice, where the polar bear will go to catch a seal.
    The Inuit hides behind a white screen waiting for the bear to make his prized kill; then he shoots the bear.

Pages 10 and 12

Mammal	**Fish**	**Bird**
bear	herring	magpie
seal	plaice	crane
doe	trout	eagle
otter	mackerel	curlew
ferret	salmon	swift
weasel	pike	ostrich
polecat	cod	buzzard
mole	perch	stork
boar	shark	raven
shrew	whiting	rook

Page 12

Capital Letters

(A)

1. at the end of every sentence there is a full stop.
   At the end of every sentence there is a full stop.
2. she is older than i.
   She is older than I.
3. yesterday helen brady was absent from school.
   Yesterday Helen Brady was absent from school.
4. i have a baby sister named jane.
   I have a baby sister named Jane.
5. pears and apples are delicious fruit.
   Pears and apples are delicious fruit.
6. peter and i went to the pictures together.
   Peter and I went to the pictures together.
7. larry daly and michael rice are cousins.
   Larry Daly and Michael Rice are cousins.
8. susan and kathleen were at the circus.
   Susan and Kathleen were at the circus.
9. every day the teacher gives us homework.
   Every day the teacher gives us homework.

(continued on next page)

Page 12 continued

10. perhaps i can help you to paint the picture.
Perhaps I can help you to paint the picture.
11. i have a friend whose name is julie.
I have a friend whose name is Julie.
12. i invited anne smith to my birthday party.
I invited Anne Smith to my birthday party.
13. the teacher asked john to collect the books.
The teacher asked John to collect the books.
14. i helped helen and christopher to lift the heavy table.
I helped Helen and Christopher to lift the heavy table.
15. my father spoke to doctor jones about my sore throat.
My father spoke to Doctor Jones about my sore throat.

(B)

1. Last wednesday the school team won the football final.
Last Wednesday the school team won the football final.
2. We have no school on good friday.
We have no school on Good Friday.
3. People all over the world celebrate christmas day.
People all over the world celebrate Christmas Day.
4. November comes between october and december.
November comes between October and December.
5. Muriel's mother made pancakes on shrove tuesday.
Muriel's mother made pancakes on Shrove Tuesday.
6. My summer holidays lasted from june to september.
My summer holidays lasted from June to September.
7. We went to the seaside for the easter bank holiday.
We went to the seaside for the Easter Bank Holiday.
8. In America the fourth of july is called independence day.
In America the fourth of July is called Independence Day.
9. April the first is called 'fools' day.
April the first is called 'Fools' Day.
10. Peter's best friend was born on new year's day.
Peter's best friend was born on New Year's Day.

Page 13

Road Safety

1. What is wrong.
2. Why it is dangerous.
3. The correct way.

1. **The two people in the picture are wearing dark-coloured clothing.**
2. **Drivers will not be able to see them, and may not slow down when they should.**
3. **Pedestrians should wear light-coloured clothing or reflective materials so they will be easily seen at night.**

1. **The girl is going to cross the road near a parked car.**
2. **The girl cannot see the road clearly and may cross in front of the moving car seen in the picture.**
3. **She should find an area clear of parked cars and use the Green Cross Code.**

1. **The lorry is overtaking the cyclist on a corner.**
2. **The lorry has had to go on to the other side of the road endangering other road users driving in this lane.**
3. **The lorry should have waited until it was in the side road before overtaking.**

1. **Three cyclists are cycling too closely together.**
2. **They will block the road and may cause each other to fall off the bicycles.**
3. **They should cycle in single file with an adequate distance between them.**

Page 14

(A) Hand Signals

1. I am going to...
   I am going to the left.

2. I am going to...
   I am going to the right.

3. I am going to...
   I am going to stop.

(B) Road Signs

1. Do not turn left.

2. You cannot go straight on.

3. Do not turn right.

4. Turn left.

5. One-way street.

6. Turn right.

7. Road veers to the left.

8. A thirty mile an hour speed limit.

9. Stop, children crossing.

The smaller signs are corresponding older versions found in copies of the question book.

Page 15

Hero Of The Wild West

Questions

1. Where was Annie Oakley born?
   Annie Oakley was born in a log cabin in Ohio.
2. Why did she go out to hunt at such an early age?
   She went out to hunt at an early age to help her mother support the family. Her father died when she was only nine years of age.
3. Who was Frank Butler?
   Frank Butler was a champion marksman and Annie's husband.
4. What nickname did Chief Sitting Bull give her?
   Chief Sitting Bull called her 'Little Sure Shot'.
5. How did she come to join the Wild West Show?
   Buffalo Bill heard of her shooting skills and invited her to join the show.
6. What trick did she perform in Berlin?
   From a distance of thirty metres, she shot a cigarette from the Crown Prince William's lips.
7. What was her best trick?
   She used a hunting knife as a mirror while she shot and hit a row of targets behind her back.
9. What have the following got in common: New York, Washington, Chicago, Dallas, Miami?
   They are all cities in the United States.
10. Try to write a sentence for each of these words: outlaw, rodeo, wigwam, ranch, sheriff, cowboy.
    Some research may be needed to answer these last two questions.

Page 16

Capital Letters

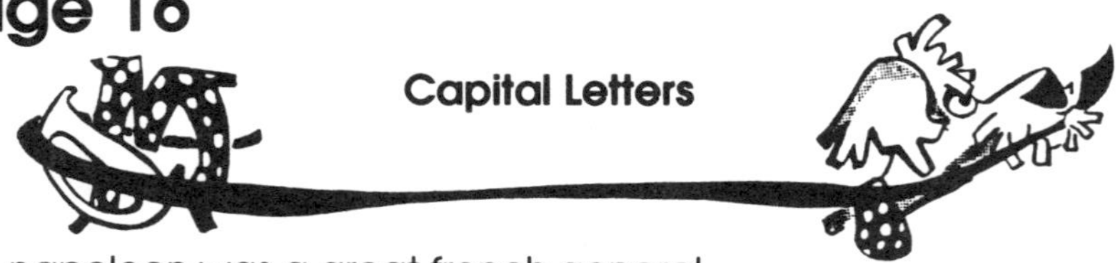

(A)

1. napoleon was a great french general.
   Napoleon was a great French general.
2. paris is the capital of france.
   Paris is the capital of France.
3. stephen king speaks fluent spanish and german.
   Stephen King speaks fluent Spanish and German.
4. the mexican bandit was captured in el paso.
   The Mexican bandit was captured in El Paso.
5. barbara's penfriend collects irish stamps.
   Barbara's penfriend collects Irish stamps.
6. many norwegian fishing trawlers fish off the coasts of canada and greenland.
   Many Norwegian fishing trawlers fish off the coasts of Canada and Greenland.
7. the italian singer sang at the music festival in wexford.
   The Italian singer sang at the music festival in Wexford.
8. frederick chopin, a polish composer, was born near warsaw.
   Frederick Chopin, a Polish composer, was born near Warsaw.
9. in the new supermarket you can buy french wine and dutch cheese.
   In the new supermarket you can buy French wine and Dutch cheese.
10. davy crockett died at the alamo.
    Davy Crockett died at the Alamo.
11. the irish team will play england in dublin on saturday.
    The Irish team will play England in Dublin on Saturday.
12. last february i received a letter from my pen-pal in india.
    Last February I received a letter from my pen-pal in India.
13. paul watkins bought a swiss watch on friday.
    Paul Watkins bought a Swiss watch on Friday.
14. the swedish girl arrived in scotland on burn's night.
    The Swedish girl arrived in Scotland on Burn's Night.
15. the person rose most admired was mother teresa of calcutta.
    The person Rose most admired was Mother Teresa of Calcutta.

Page 16 continued

(B)

Country	**People**	**Language**
Belgium	Belgian	Flemish, French
Canada	**Canadian**	**English, French**
Denmark	**Danish**	**Danish**
England	**English**	**English**
France	**French**	**French**
Ireland	**Irish**	**English, Gaelic**
Germany	**German**	**German**
Holland	**Dutch**	**Dutch**
Poland	**Polish**	**Polish**
Portugal	**Portuguese**	**Portuguese**
Russia	**Russian**	**Russian**
Scotland	**Scottish**	**English**
Spain	**Spanish**	**Spanish**
Sweden	**Swedish**	**Swedish**
Switzerland	**Swiss**	**German, French**

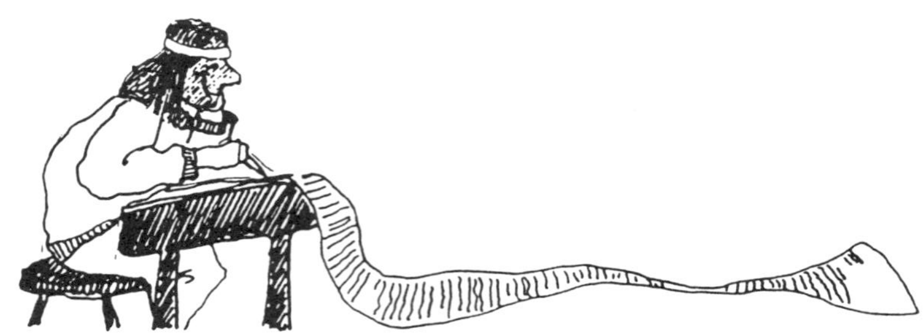

Page 17

The Jumbo Jet

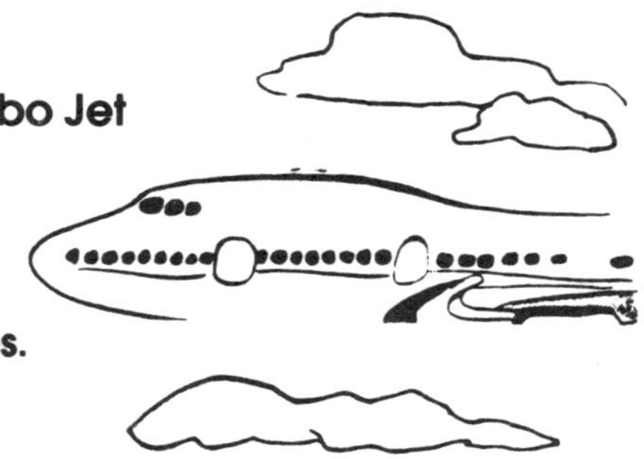

Questions

1. How heavy is the Jumbo Jet?
   A Jumbo Jet weighs 300 tonnes.
2. How much fuel does it carry?
   It carries 214 000 litres of fuel.
3. How many passengers can it carry?
   It can carry 416 passengers.
4. What height and speed does it reach?
   At 10 600 metres, the Boeing 747 will cruise along at a speed of 912 kilometres an hour (560 mph).
5. What did a Jumbo Jet once meet with on its way to New Zealand?
   The aircraft met with a thick, deadly cloud of dust and ash thrown into the sky by a volcano.
6. Why do you think its engines cut out?
   They had been blocked by the ash.
7. What did the pilot do?
   He put the plane into a glide and turned back for the airport.
8. What have Heathrow, Gatwick, Luton and Stansted all got in common?
9. Who were the Wright Brothers?
   Some research may be needed for these last two questions.

Page 19

The Oldest Living Thing In The World

Questions

1. How did the Sequoia tree get its name?
   It was named after Sikwayi, a Cherokee Indian, who invented a system of writing for his tribe.
2. How high and wide is the Giant Sequoia?
   It can grow to a height of 100 metres, and its trunk is so wide that roads have even been tunnelled through a number without any difficulty.
3. How is the Sequoia able to gain protection from enemy insects?
   The bark is so thick that it can easily resist the attacks of chewing insects.
4. What is the oldest living thing in the world?
   A tree called the Bristlecone Pine, native to the USA.
5. How is it possible to date a tree?
   You can date a tree by counting its rings.
6. Why are some rings found to be bigger than others?
   Some are bigger than others because the tree grew more in some years than in others.
7. What kind of information can be got from these ancient trees?
   By studying the trees' rings, it is possible to build up a good picture of the weather and the growing conditions of past ages.
8. What are the main uses of trees?
9. List the names of all the trees you know.
10. Can you explain the difference between an evergreen and a deciduous tree?
   Some research may be needed for these last three questions.

Page 20

Over-Used Words

Said

1. Patrick *said* that the weather was terrible.
   Patrick complained that the weather was terrible.
2. "Will you give me a loan of your rubber?" *said* Peter.
   "Will you give me a loan of your rubber?" asked Peter.
3. Kate *said* a secret in my ear.
   Kate whispered a secret in my ear.
4. "Please bring us to the zoo," *said* the children.
   "Please bring us to the zoo," begged the children.
5. "The train is coming," *said* Grandad.
   "The train is coming," shouted Grandad.
6. Mary *said* a story in class yesterday.
   Mary told a story in class yesterday.
7. "Stay in bed for the rest of the week," *said* the doctor.
   "Stay in bed for the rest of the week," advised the doctor.
8. The general *said* that the army was to retreat.
   The general ordered that the army was to retreat.

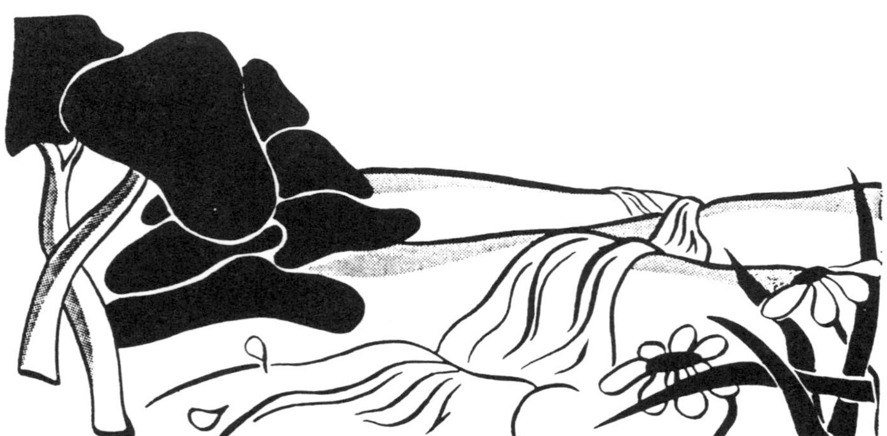

Page 21

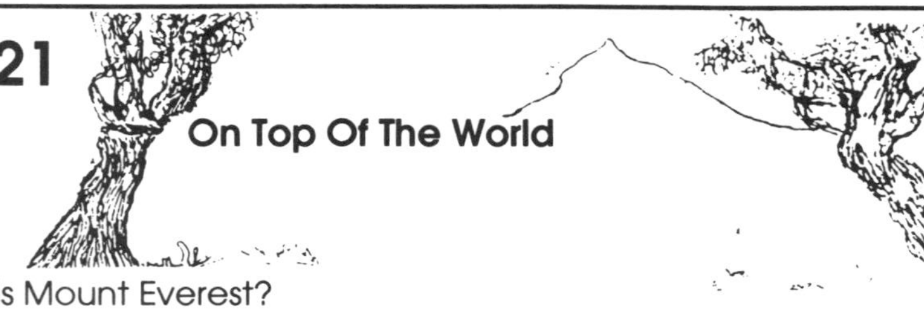

On Top Of The World

Questions

1. Where is Mount Everest?
   It stands on the border of Tibet and Nepal.
2. How high is it?
   It is 8 848 metres (5.5 miles) to its summit.
3. Give four reasons why Everest is such a difficult mountain to climb.
   Everest is such a difficult mountain to climb because of the lack of oxygen at high levels, fierce snowstorms, dangerous ice and bottomless chasms.
4. How many expeditions had failed to climb the mountain by 1953?
   At least ten expeditions had failed to climb the mountain.
5. What was the plan of the next expedition?
   They planned to set up eight camps along the way to the summit. Then two men would be chosen to make the final climb to the summit.
6. Who were chosen to make the final attempt on the summit?
   Edmund Hillary and Tenzing Norgay made the final attempt on the summit.
7. What were they delighted to see on the morning of May 29th 1953?
   On the morning of May 29th 1953 they were delighted to see calm and sunny weather.
8. List the qualities needed to make a good mountain climber.
9. Write a paragraph about an exciting sport you would like to try.
10. Try to find out the name, height and location of Britain's tallest mountain.
   Some research may be needed for these last three questions.

Page 22

Singular and Plural

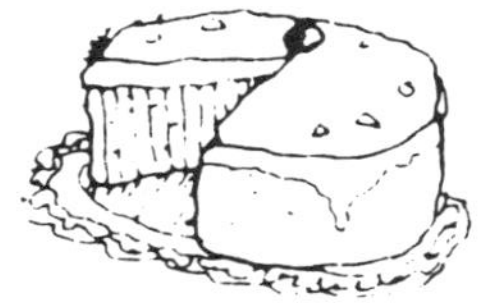

(A)

1. The *boy* put the *cake* in the *oven*.
   The **boys** put the **cakes** in the **ovens**.
2. The *farmer* lifted the *rock* from the *field*.
   The **farmers** lifted the **rocks** from the **fields**.
3. The *cook* prepared the *dish* in the kitchen.
   The **cooks** prepared the **dishes** in the kitchen.
4. The *bishop* visited the *church* in the *town*.
   The **bishops** visited the **churches** in the **towns**.
5. His *uncle* gave him the *watch*.
   His **uncles** gave him the **watches**.
6. The *soldier* loaded the *gun* with the *bullet*.
   The **soldiers** loaded the **guns** with the **bullets**.
7. The *bird* flew from the *bush*.
   The **birds** flew from the **bushes**.
8. The *plumber* fixed the *pipe* in the *cottage*.
   The **plumbers** fixed the **pipes** in the **cottages**.
9. The *pirate* attacked the *ship* near the *island*.
   The **pirates** attacked the **ships** near the **islands**.
10. The *class* found the *shell* on the *beach*.
    The **classes** found the **shells** on the **beaches**.

(B)

1. He ate the *biscuit* on the *tray*.
   He ate the **biscuits** on the **trays**.
2. The *train* sped through the *valley*.
   The **trains** sped through the **valleys**.
3. She left the *key* in the *pocket*.
   She left the **keys** in the **pockets**.
4. He bought the *tie* and the *jersey*.
   He bought the **ties** and the **jerseys**.
5. The *ray* of light came through the *window*.
   The **rays** of light came through the **windows**.

Page 22 continued

6. Snow covered the *roof* and *chimney*.
   Snow covered the **roofs** and **chimneys**.
7. The *boat* sailed away from the *quay*.
   The **boats** sailed away from the **quays**.
8. The *horse* and *jockey* cleared the *fence*.
   The **horses** and **jockeys** cleared the **fences**.
9. The *cow* and the *donkey* ate the *vegetable*.
   The **cows** and the **donkeys** ate the **vegetables**.
10. They served the *turkey* at the *dinner*.
    They served the **turkeys** at the **dinners**.

(C)

1. The ladies read the books on the trains.
   The lady read the book on the train.
2. The dentists extracted the children's teeth.
   The dentist extracted the child's tooth.
3. The enemies lived in far away countries.
   The enemy lived in a far away country.
4. The foxes ate the salmon.
   The fox ate the salmon.
5. The fish were swimming in the deep pools.
   The fish was swimming in the deep pool.
6. The potatoes were served with fish.
   The potato was served with fish.
7. The shops sell pliers and shears.
   The shop sells pliers and shears.
8. The farmers put the turkeys in sheds.
   The farmer put a turkey in the shed.
9. The brushes were left on the roofs.
   The brush was left on the roof.
10. The husbands and wives played with the babies.
    The husband and wife played with the baby.

Page 23

Silver Streak

Questions

1. What is a redd?
   This is the nest in which a female salmon lays her eggs.
2. When is the young salmon called a parr?
   When it develops stripes it is called a parr.
3. Why does the smolt float down with its tail first?
   This prevents water from flooding its gills which would cause it to drown.
4. What does the salmon feed on at sea?
   Their diet consists of shrimps and prawns.
5. What is the 'salmon run'?
   This is the salmon's return journey from the sea to its place of birth.
6. How far can a salmon travel in a day?
   It can travel up to twenty kilometres in a day.

Page 24

Nouns

(A)

1. The horse galloped down the field.
   Horse and field.
2. Mary hurt her elbow when she fell off her bike.
   Mary, elbow and bike.
3. The panda was caught in a forest in China.
   Panda, forest and China.
4. The waiter put the coffee, milk and sugar on the table.
   Waiter, coffee, milk, sugar and table.
5. The soldiers charged when the corporal blew the bugle.
   Soldiers, corporal and bugle.
6. The match was played before a large crowd at Croke Park.
   Match, crowd and Croke Park.
7. The hawk had a nest with two eggs at the top of the cliff.
   Hawk, nest, eggs and cliff.
8. He spotted a bright diamond flashing in the rock.
   Diamond and rock.
9. Huge waves crashed against the rocks below the lighthouse.
   Waves, rocks and lighthouse.
10. Jesus was born in a stable at Bethlehem.
    Jesus, stable and Bethlehem.

(C)

1. A person who gives lessons...
   a teacher.
2. The place where an Eskimo lives...
   an igloo.
3. The animal which tempted Adam and Eve...
   a snake.
4. A person who fights fires...
   a firefighter.
5. The place where a clown performs...
   a circus.
6. The animal known as the 'king of the jungle'...
   the lion.
7. A thing which is used for measuring time...
   a clock/watch.
8. A person who travels in space...
   an astronaut.
9. An animal with a very long neck...
   a giraffe.
10. A place where paintings are put on display...
    a gallery.

Page 27

A Dinner of Smells

Questions

1. Why was the poor man 'tired and very hungry'?
   He was tired and very hungry because he had not eaten all day.
2. What caused him to stop outside the restaurant?
   He stopped to sniff the delicious toad being cooked inside.
3. What is a Quadi?
   A Quadi is a judge in a Muslim court.
4. What is a mullah?
   A mullah is a person who is knowledgeable about the Muslim faith and law.
5. Why didn't the restaurant owner want the poor man outside the restaurant?
   The restaurant owner did not want a poor man smelling his fine and expensive food.
6. How much could the poor man afford to pay?
   He could afford nothing.
7. What tells us that the restaurant owner was a cruel and mean man?
   Any appropriate answer should be acceptable.
8. Was the Quadi a fair man?
   Any appropriate answer should be acceptable.

Page 28

Nouns

1. Rabbits dig burrows in the ground.
   Rabbits, burrows and ground.
2. My dog lives in a kennel.
   Dog and kennel.
3. The bullfrog leaped into the pond.
   Bullfrog and pond.
4. There are many giraffes and lions in Africa.
   Giraffes, lions and Africa.
5. The eagle has a nest in the mountains.
   Eagle, nest and mountains.
6. Honeybees make honey in hives.
   Honeybees, honey and hives.
7. John Smith bought a donkey and a goat.
   John Smith, donkey and goat.
8. The sheepdog buried a bone in the garden.
   Sheepdog, bone and garden.
9. The spider spun a web in the garage.
   Spider, web and garage.
10. The wasp stung Mary on the nose.
    Wasp, Mary and nose.

Page 31

The Eel

Questions

1. Where do eels breed?
   Eels breed in the Sargasso Sea.
2. What is a young eel called?
   Young eels are called elvers.
3. How do eels breathe?
   They breathe mainly through the tiny blood vessels in their damp skin.
4. Where do they spend most of their lives?
   They spend most of their lives in rivers, streams, lakes and ponds.
5. How does the female eel make her way inland?
   She wriggles, glides and crawls over dams, waterfalls, marshy lands and through sewerage pipes to reach her destination.
6. Name some of the eel's enemies.
   Otters and herons are two of the eel's enemies.
7. What do eels feed on?
   Eels feed on water insects, snails, smaller fish and garbage.
8. How many years does the female eel remain inland?
   The female eel remains inland for seven to fifteen years.

Page 32

Sounds and Movements

(A)

1. The eagle **screams** and **swoops**.
2. The owl **hoots** and **flits**.
3. The robin **chirps** and **hops**.
4. The crow **caws** and **flaps its wings**.
5. The pigeon **coos** and **flutters**.
6. The duck **quacks** and **waddles**.
7. The lark **sings** and **soars**.
8. The hen **cackles** and **struts**.
9. The sparrow **chirps** and **hops**.
10. The seagull **screams** and **glides**.

(B)

1. The horse **neighs** and **gallops**.
2. The dog **barks** and **runs**.
3. The wolf **howls** and **lopes**.
4. The bull **bellows** and **charges**.
5. The pig **grunts** and **trots**.
6. The lion **roars** and **prowls**.
7. The monkey **chatters** and **climbs**.
8. The lamb **bleats** and **frisks**.
9. The bear **growls** and **lumbers**.
10. The mouse **squeaks** and **scampers**.

Page 32 continued

(C)

1. The **beat** of a drum.
2. The **rumble** of a train.
3. The **hoot** of a horn.
4. The **chime** of a clock.
5. The **screech** of brakes.
6. The **whirring** of wings.
7. The **crack** of a whip.
8. The **jingle** of coins.
9. The **lapping** of water.
10. The rush of **feet**.
11. The swish of **skirts**.
12. The wail of a **siren**.
13. The sizzling of **sausages**.
14. The pitter-patter of **raindrops**.
15. The ping of a **bullet**.
16. The popping of **corks**.

Page 36

The Hedgehog

Questions

1. How do you think the hedgehog got his name?
   The hedgehog got his name because he lives in hedgerows and grunts and snorts around searching for food like a pig.
2. How does he defend himself?
   He defends himself by curling up into a ball and extending his spines.
3. What enemies has he?
   Two of his enemies are the fox and the badger.
4. Where would you expect to find hedgehogs?
   You would expect to find hedgehogs in ditches, hedgerows and gardens.
5. How are the spines useful to the hedgehog?
   The hedgehog can use its spines for defence and for collecting food.
6. What is the hedgehog's favourite food?
   The hedgehog has many favourite foods including crab apples and snakes.
7. What does he hunt by night?
   At night he hunts for snails, beetles, woodlice, slugs and grubs.
8. When are young hedgehogs born?
   Young hedgehogs are born twice a year. The first brood is born in early summer and the second one is born in the autumn.
9. Why are baby hedgehogs defenceless?
   They are defenceless because they cannot curl up into a ball and they have only a few rubbery spines.
10. How does a hedgehog kill a viper?
    He spikes the snake's head and fangs and bites it on the back of the neck until it dies.

(A)

1. hedgehog, hyena, horse, hare, hippopotamus.
   hare, hedgehog, hippopotamus, horse, hyena.
2. buffalo, badger, beaver, bat, bear.
   badger, bat, bear, beaver, buffalo.
3. mule, monkey, moose, mole, mouse.
   mole, monkey, moose, mouse, mule.
4. stoat, sheep, squirrel, skunk, seal.
   seal, sheep, skunk, squirrel, stoat.
5. gorilla, giraffe, goat, gazelle.
   gazelle, giraffe, goat, gorilla.

Pages 37 and 38

Nature Trail

Across
3. Squirrel
5. Acorn
8. Swallow
10. Beetle
12. Grasshopper
16. Snail
17. Duck
18. Butterfly
19. Mushroom

Down
1. Swan
2. Frog
4. Ladybird
6. Caterpillar
7. Bee
9. Wasp
11. Lizard
13. Holly
14. Robin
15. Ant

The Frog

(A)
1. A frog **croaks.**
2. A frog eats **insects.**
3. A frog has webbed **feet**.
4. A frog is smaller than an **alligator**.
5. A frog is an **amphibian**.
6. A baby frog is called a **tadpole**.
7. A grown frog has **lungs**.
8. A frog cannot **fly**.
9. A grown frog has no **tail**.
10. A frog's eggs are called **spawn**.

(B)

1.	A girl's dress.	**Frock**.
2.	Apples, pears, and bananas.	**Fruit**.
3.	Once a tadpole.	**Frog**.
4.	A French coin.	**Franc**.
5.	The opposite of 'stale'.	**Fresh**.
6.	A week day.	**Friday**.
8.	A brown spot on your face.	**Freckle**.
9.	The opposite of 'back'.	**Front**.
10.	Paris is the capital of this country.	**France**.

Page 41

William Tell

Questions

1. Where did the events in the story take place?
   The events took place in the village of Altdorf in Switzerland.
2. Who was Gessler?
   He was the Austrian governor of Altdorf.
3. How did he try to humiliate the Swiss people?
   He tried to humiliate them by ordering them to kneel and bow before his hat.
4. What was the name of William Tell's son?
   William Tell's son was called Jimmy.
5. How did Tell display his skill in archery?
   Tell shot an apple which he had placed on his son's head.
6. What was the reason for the second arrow?
   The second arrow would have been used to kill Gessler if Jimmy had been injured.
7. How did the tyrant Gessler die?
   William Tell shot Gessler.
8. How do you know that Tell was an expert sailor?
   During a terrible storm, he took the helm of a boat and steered accurately to shore so that he could make his escape.

1. needle and **thread**.
2. hammer and **tongs**.
3. scissors and **paper**.
4. spade and **fork**.
5. lock and **key**.
6. knife and **fork**.
7. pen and **paper**.
8. hook and **eye**.
9. pepper and **salt**.
10. iron and **steel**.
11. soap and **water**.
12. sea and **sand**.

Page 42

Confusing Words

(A) 'Two' 'Too' 'To'

1. Jane found it ... difficult ... crawl between the ... legs of the chair.
   Jane found it **too** difficult **to** crawl between the **two** legs of the chair.
2. She went ... the bathroom, turned on the ... taps and flooded the place.
   She went **to** the bathroom, turned on the **two** taps and flooded the place.
3. I was ... frightened ... tell mother the story.
   I was **too** frightened **to** tell mother the story.
4. When she broke the ... cups, Dad spoke gently ... her, but her mother was not ... pleased.
   When she broke the **two** cups, Dad spoke gently **to** her, but her mother was not **too** pleased.
5. There was ... much jam on the slice of bread.
   There was **too** much jam on the slice of bread.
6. The doll was ... expensive ... buy.
   The doll was **too** expensive **to** buy.
7. It was ... early for the baby ... go ... bed.
   It was **too** early for the baby **to** go **to** bed.
8. During her ... weeks in hospital, she was ... sick ... suck lollipops.
   During her **two** weeks in hospital, she was **too** sick **to** suck lollipops.
9. The ... of us loved ... tug and pull the pillow.
   The **two** of us loved **to** tug and pull the pillow.
10. Jane made ... much noise with the ... spoons.
    Jane made **too** much noise with the **two** spoons.

Page 42 continued

(B) 'Stood' and 'Standing'

1. I was ... by the door when the accident occurred.
   I was **standing** by the door when the accident occurred.
2. He ... up and walked towards the window.
   He **stood** up and walked towards the window.
3. The statue was ... in the corner.
   The statue was **standing** in the corner.
4. They were ... still when the National Anthem was played.
   They were **standing** still when the National Anthem was played.
5. The police will be ... close by.
   The police will be **standing** close by.
6. You would see if you ... on the ladder.
   You would see if you **stood** on the ladder.
7. The audience gave a ... ovation.
   The audience gave a **standing** ovation.

(C) 'Has' and 'Have'

1. The pups ... meat for dinner but the cat ... fish.
   The pups **have** meat for dinner but the cat **has** fish.
2. We ... to meet the lady who ... the books.
   We **have** to meet the lady who **has** the books.
3. A whale ... lungs but a fish ... gills.
   A whale **has** lungs but a fish **has** gills.
4. The girls ... measles and the boys ... the mumps.
   The girls **have** measles and the boys **have** the mumps.
5. The soldiers ... guns and their captains ... swords.
   The soldiers **have** guns and their captains **have** swords.
6. ... you heard the orders he ... given us?
   Have you heard the orders he **has** given us?
7. ... she seen the present you ... bought?
   Has she seen the present you **have** bought?

Page 44

Unusual Birds

Questions

1. Where would you find the humming bird?
   The hummingbird is found in the tropical regions of North and South America and in Cuba.
2. Why does it beat its wings so rapidly?
   It beats its wings so rapidly so that it can remain in the same position, fly backwards or even rise straight like a helicopter.
3. How does it build its nest?
   A mass of grasses, mosses and fibres are woven together with strands of cobwebs, to form a tiny nest about the size of a walnut shell.
4. How does the mother feed her young?
   She regurgitates (throws up) the sweet nectar from her stomach into the nestlings' mouths.
5. What record does the Arctic Tern hold?
   The Arctic Tern holds the record for champion long-distance traveller.
6. What record does the humming bird hold?
   The humming bird holds the record for being the smallest bird in the world.

Wordsearch

Parrot
Kestrel
Duck
Gull
Cuckoo
Thrush
Owl
Swift
Wren
Lark
Vulture
Eagle

N	O	C	**K**	**P**	**A**	**R**	**R**	**O**	**T**
E	**A**	**G**	**L**	**E**	R	T	T	S	**H**
E	**D**	**U**	**C**	**K**	**S**	H	L	P	**R**
M	O	**L**	**C**	**V**	D	**T**	V	R	**U**
M	V	**L**	E	**U**	Q	F	**R**	B	**S**
S	**S**	R	P	**L**	**C**	A	A	**E**	**H**
O	**W**	**L**	F	**T**	**A**	**K**	S	H	**L**
O	**I**	T	H	**U**	B	**R**	**O**	B	M
U	**F**	H	**W**	**R**	**E**	**N**	**K**	**O**	L
V	**T**	T	L	**E**	Z	Y	X	B	T

Page 45

Adjectives

(A)

1. Their **tired** eyes looked out across the **vast** desert.
2. Our **simple** but **clever** plan was to hide in the **wooden** barn.
3. The **ugly** witch rode across the **dark** sky on a **magical** broomstick.
4. They tied a **long** string to a **red rosy** apple.
5. On Hallowe'en we dressed up as **ugly** goblins and **dangerous** demons.
6. The **hungry** thrush fed on a **fat, juicy** worm.
7. The **little** girl's pet rabbit loved its **cosy** new home.
8. The **first** train was **fast** and **comfortable**.
9. The **thin** ice cracked under the weight of the **heavy** skater.
10. The **silver** salmon slept in the **deep, dark** pool.

(B)

The Aitkin family rose early on the **first** morning of their holiday in Wales. The weather was **warm** and **sunny** – a **perfect** day for a **nice** picnic at the seaside. The **happy** and **excited** children helped their parents prepare a **big** feast of **tasty** sandwiches and **home-made** cakes. After a **quick** breakfast they set off on foot for a **small sandy** beach about a mile from their **thatched** cottage. Already, the **clear, blue** sky was filled with the **sweet**, **joyful** song of **tiny** larks. As they strolled down the **dusty** road, their **eager** eyes gazed upon the **broad, calm** ocean.

(C)

He was an **old** man and he lived in the **big** house next to ours. He was very **kind** to the birds during the **cold** months of winter. Each morning he used to bring them **small** morsels of **soft** bread. The **shivering** birds used to perch on his **outstretched** arm and eat the crumbs of bread. It was a very **touching** sight to see this **generous** man with his **feathery** friends around him.

Page 46

Extending Sentences

(B)

1. The bull chased him. Luckily he escaped.
   The bull chased him but luckily he escaped.
2. The policeman blew his whistle. The man stopped.
   The policeman blew his whistle and the man stopped.
3. It is raining today. It was fine yesterday.
   It is raining today but it was fine yesterday.
4. Our cat has a tail. A Manx cat has no tail.
   Our cat has a tail but a Manx cat has no tail.
5. The player scored a goal. The crowd cheered.
   The player scored a goal and the crowd cheered.
6. I knocked loudly on the door. She did not open it.
   I knocked loudly on the door but she did not open it.
7. A large fire burned in the grate. The room was warm.
   A large fire burned in the grate and the room was warm.
8. The cow was milked. The calves were fed.
   The cow was milked and the calves were fed.

Page 48

Greece, Home Of The Olympics

Questions

1. Where were the Olympic Games held?
   The Olympic Games were held in Olympia, Greece.
2. Why did the athletes travel early to the games?
   The athletes arrived early so that they could train for the events.
3. What did the valley at Olympia look like at the time of the games?
   The valley was a sea of little white tents.
4. Describe the chariot race.
   Competitors rode in two-wheeled chariots drawn by teams of four horses. The race was run over a distance of nine kilometres.
5. What would happen on the afternoon of the third day of the games?
   During the afternoon of the third day, one hundred cattle were sacrificed to please the gods.
6. Which were the most popular events of the Olympics?
   The most popular events were the boxing and wrestling.
7. What did the winners receive?
   The winners received a simple olive wreath.
8. Write out the timetable of events for the four days of the Olympics.
   An appropriate timetable should be acceptable.

Page 49

Question Marks

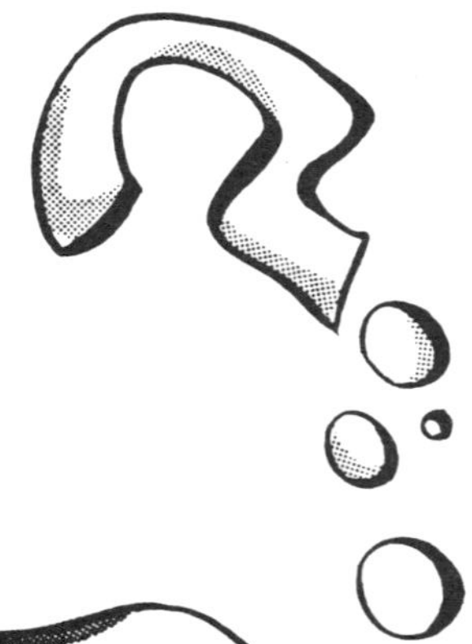

(A)

1. how old are you
   How old are you?
2. why is the school closed today
   Why is the school closed today?
3. where is the circus
   Where is the circus?
4. who won the race
   Who won the race?
5. when is the bus coming
   When is the bus coming?
6. whose coat is this
   Whose coat is this?
7. what did she buy
   What did she buy?
8. which house is yours
   Which house is yours?
9. shall we go shopping
   Shall we go shopping?
10. is this your coat
   Is this your coat?

(B)

1. She is twelve years of age.
   How old is she?
2. He left the room because he was angry.
   Why did he leave the room?
3. The train arrived at six o'clock.
   What time did the train arrive?
4. Honeybees live in hives.
   Where do honeybees live?
5. Tom's horse won the race.
   Where did Tom's horse come in the race?
6. The inspector came by car.
   How did the inspector get here?
7. It is my pen.
   Whose pen is this?
8. The runaway horse jumped the wall.
   How did the runaway horse escape?
9. Our new teacher decorated the room.
   Who decorated the room?
10. She decided to buy the yellow frock.
   What colour frock did she decide to buy?

Page 51

Sammy Snail

Questions

1. Where would you expect to find snails?
   Snails live under stones and vegetation.
2. Where did the snail get his shell?
   His shell is part of his body and grows with him.
3. How can he travel over rough and dry ground?
   He lays down a trail of slime to help him glide over rough and dry ground.
4. What kind of food does he like to eat?
   He likes to eat green cabbage leaves, young plants and garden fruits.
5. Why do gardeners dislike snails?
   Gardeners dislike snails because they eat their plants.
6. What enemies has he?
   One of his enemies is the thrush.
7. How does the little creature protect his eyes?
   The little creature protects his eyes by rolling them down his hollow tentacles.
8. Give words to describe the movements of the snail.
   Some examples may be: glide, slow, slimy.
9. How might a snail escape from a sealed cardboard box?
   Some research may be needed.
10. Which of these soft-bodied creatures have shells?
   crab, worm, oyster, slug, periwinkle, starfish, octopus, clam, scallop, squid.
   crab, oyster, periwinkle, clam, scallop.
11. Explain the following phrases.
   i) going at a snail's pace.
   moving as slow as a snail.
   ii) to be a bookworm.
   always reading books.

Pages 52 and 53

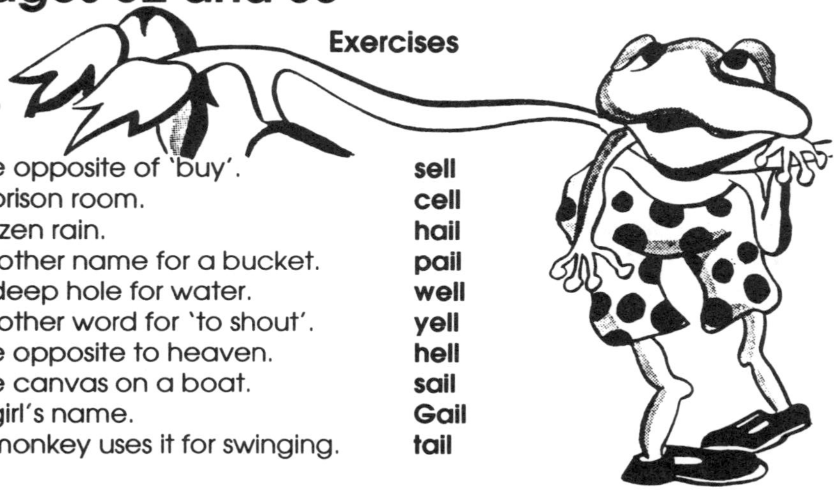

Exercises

(A)

The opposite of 'buy'.	**sell**
A prison room.	**cell**
Frozen rain.	**hail**
Another name for a bucket.	**pail**
A deep hole for water.	**well**
Another word for 'to shout'.	**yell**
The opposite to heaven.	**hell**
The canvas on a boat.	**sail**
A girl's name.	**Gail**
A monkey uses it for swinging.	**tail**

(A)

1. salmon, trout, minnow, shark.
   minnow, trout, salmon, shark.
2. alligator, frog, penguin, newt.
   newt, frog, penguin, alligator.
3. elephant, mouse, fox, rabbit.
   mouse, rabbit, fox, elephant.
4. duck, swan, seal, duckling.
   duckling, duck, swan, seal.
5. zebra, monkey, kangaroo, camel.
   monkey, kangaroo, zebra, camel.

(C)

F	**Fr**	**Fl**	**Ph (f sound)**	**...gh (f sound)**
five	Friday	flag	phone	rough
farm	**fraction**	**flash**	**Philip**	**cough**
fun	**freckles**	**flower**	**photo**	**enough**
fork	**freeze**	**flask**	**phrase**	**laugh**
finger	**frame**	**flock**	**phantom**	**tough**
father	**friend**	**flood**	**elephant**	**trough**

Pages 53 and 54

(D)

1. A caterpillar is a young **butterfly or moth.**
2. A fry is a young **fish**.
3. A grub is a young **insect.**
4. A tadpole is a young **frog**.
5. A lamb is a young **sheep**.
6. A cygnet is a young **swan**.
7. A kitten is a young **cat**.
8. A calf is a young **cow**.
9. A gosling is a young **goose**.
10. A leveret is a young **hare**.
11. A nestling is a young **bird**.
12. A piglet is a young **pig**.
13. An elver is a young **eel**.
14. A parr is a young **salmon**.

The King's Problem

Questions

1. Where and when was Archimedes born?
   Archimedes was born in Sicily, around the year 285BC.
2. Why is he famous today?
   He is remembered as a great scientist and inventor.
3. What was the king's problem?
   He wanted to know whether his crown was made of pure gold.
4. Why did he turn to Archimedes for help?
   He turned to Archimedes for help because he could not prove that the mixture was not gold as it looked like gold.
5. What happened when Archimedes got into his bath?
   The bath was full to the brim and when he got into it it overflowed.
6. Why did he shout 'Eureka'?
   He shouted 'Eureka' because he had solved the king's problem.
7. What discovery had he made?
   He discovered that any object put into water will raise the water by an amount exactly equal to the bulk of the object.
8. What do you think the king did when it was proved he had been cheated?
   Any appropriate answer will do.
9. List the names of any metals you know.
   Some metals are silver, iron, copper, aluminium.
10. Write down what you know about any great inventor or scientist.
    Some research may be needed.

Page 55

Verbs

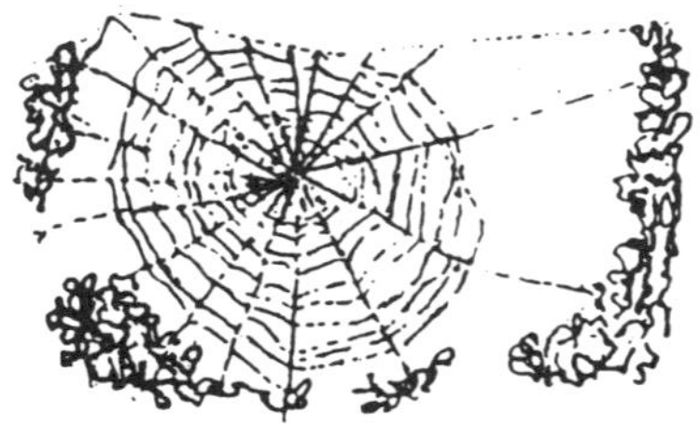

(A)

1. House spiders **weave** cobwebs.
2. The squirrel **built** a drey.
3. The otter **caught** a fat waterhen.
4. The cat is **purring** near the fire.
5. **Run** before the bull **charges**.
6. I shall **feed** the robins.
7. A monkey **chatters** and an ape **gibbers**.
8. At night the owl **hoots** in the forest.
9. Tom will **train** the horse for the big race.
10. The tiger **chased** the wild goat.

(C)

1. Peter **loved** the monkeys but Mary ... the gorillas.
   Peter loved the monkeys but Mary **hated** the gorillas.
2. He **sold** his old bicycle and ... a new one.
   He sold his old bicycle and **bought** a new one.
3. When the bull **appeared** at the fence the children ... quickly.
   When the bull appeared at the fence the children **disappeared** quickly.
4. **Shut** the door and ... the window.
   Shut the door and **open** the window.
5. I **remember** people's names but I ... their addresses.
   I remember people's names but I **forget** their addresses.
6. The elephant **raised** its leg and ... its trunk.
   The elephant raised its leg and **lowered** its trunk.
7. We **commenced** the exam in the morning and ... it in the afternoon.
   We commenced the exam in the morning and **finished** it in the afternoon.

Page 58

Monsters from the Past

Questions

1. What is the meaning of the word dinosaur?
   The word dinosaur means 'terrible lizard'.
2. When did they live on this Earth?
   They lived on this Earth millions of years ago.
3. Describe the world at that time.
   At that time the world was covered with great forests and swamps. Towering trees and ferns, some over 30 metres high, grew all the year round.
5. How does a dinosaur compare in size with an elephant?
   Dinosaurs could be three or four times the size of a large elephant.
6. Which one of the dinosaurs was king of the forest?
   Tyrannosaurus Rex was king of the forest.
7. Who was his great enemy?
   His great enemy was the Triceratops.
8. Where did the fight take place?
   The fight took place near the edge of a big swamp.
9. How did Triceratops defend himself?
   He defended himself using his three horns as weapons to spike his enemy.
10. Why do you think he lost the fight?
    Any appropriate answer will do.

Page 59

'A' or 'An'

(A)

1. We saw ... unusual crocodile near ... marshy swamp.
   We saw **an** unusual crocodile near **a** marshy swamp.

2. I watched ... enormous reptile kill ... elephant in ... cave.
   I watched **an** enormous reptile kill **an** elephant in **a** cave.

3. She saw ... swarm of giant ants attacking ... nest of cockroaches.
   She saw **a** swarm of giant ants attacking **a** nest of cockroaches.

4. ... huge frog, with ... long tail, leaped into ... deep hole.
   A huge frog, with **a** long tail, leaped into **a** deep hole.

5. ... eight-tonne dinosaur had ... small brain.
   An eight-tonne dinosaur had **a** small brain.

6. ... Iguanodon laid ... egg the size of ... football.
   An Iguanodon laid **an** egg the size of **a** football.

7. ... giant toad swallowed ... large fly.
   A giant toad swallowed **a** large fly.

8. ... Allosaurus was ... giant dinosaur.
   An Allosaurus was **a** giant dinosaur.

9. ... Archaeopteryx was ... flying bird.
   An Archaeopteryx was **a** flying bird.

10. I sent ... old dagger to ... friend in the museum.
    I sent **an** old dagger to **a** friend in the museum.

Page 60

Verbs

(A)

1. The busy bee **flitted** across the room.
2. The horrid beetle **crawled** under the stone.
3. The pretty butterfly **hovered** near the rose bushes.
4. The timid snail **glided** along the damp grass.
5. The house spider **scurried** into its web.
6. The fat worm **wriggled** into its burrow.
7. The prickly hedgehog **prodded** the dog with its spines.
8. The golden eagle **trapped** the lamb in its talons.
9. The croaking bullfrog **leaped** into the deep pool.
10. The brown hen **pecked** the pan of oats.

(B)

1. He **knew** the man. He did not ... the stranger.
   He knew the man. He did not **know** the stranger.
2. She **wrote** a letter to her friend. She has ... to her friend.
   She wrote a letter to her friend. She has **written** to her friend.
3. He **went** for a drive. He has ... to visit his aunt.
   He went for a drive. He has **gone** to visit his aunt.
4. He **came** late last night. I did not know if he would ...
   He came late last night. I did not know if he would **come**.
5. He **gave** her a lovely present. He has ... her a new car.
   He gave her a lovely present. He has **given** her a new car.
6. The hungry dog **ate** the meat. The dog had not ... for days.
   The hungry dog ate the meat. The dog had not **eaten** for days.
7. He **flew** to London. He had never ... by plane.
   He flew to London. He had never **flown** by plane.
8. She **tore** up my notes. My coat was badly ...
   She tore up my notes. My coat was badly **torn**.
9. The thief **hid** behind the tree. He had ... the jewels in a safe place.
   The thief hid behind the tree. He had **hidden** the jewels in a safe place.
10. I **forgot** the man's name. I had not ... my first meeting with him.
    I forgot the man's name. I had not **forgotten** my first meeting with him.

Page 60 continued

(C)

1. Peter saw a colony of bats as he walked **past** the graveyard.
2. When the bat flew **past**, Margaret screamed in terror.
3. The proud eagle swooped **past** her nest.
4. Many days **passed** before my racing pigeon returned home.
5. They were attacked by vampire bats as they **passed** through the cave.
6. The loathsome bat **passed** on the dreaded disease, rabies.
7. At half **past** eight the bus **passed** by my house.
8. It flew **past** in wide circles and **passed** over the marshy swamp.
9. I **passed** many happy hours watching the salmon leaping over the falls.

Page 61

'...ing'

1. I saw a buck rabbit **nibbling** a juicy lettuce leaf.
2. Mary heard the bull frogs **croaking** in the marshy pond.
3. The **howling** wind whistled through the keyhole.
4. The **blossoming** daffodils unfolded their golden frilly bonnets.
5. The silver grey stallion went **galloping** across the field.
6. The **bubbling** stream gurgled over rocks and boulders.
7. The warm sun was **shining** brightly in the clear blue sky.
8. The **crackling** of firewood frightened the timid squirrel.
9. The birds were **whistling** merrily in the hedgerows and bushes.
10. The donkey was **braying** and the horse was **neighing**.
11. The **lapping** waters washed the barren rocks.
12. The father oiled the **creaking** hinges.
13. We heard the **rattling** of chains and the **clattering** of hooves as we passed the graveyard.
14. I was aroused by the **clanking** of dishes and the **shuffling** of feet in the kitchen.
15. The **screaming** seagulls glided over the waves.

Page 62

Unusual Fish

1. Where would you find the piranha?
   The fish lives in the Amazon and Orinoco Rivers of South America.
2. How can such a small fish as the piranha be so dangerous?
   They have razor teeth and travel in large schools enabling them to attack other animals many times their size.
3. What does the archer fish feed on?
   The archer fish feeds on insects.
4. How does it catch its victim?
   It fires a jet of water from its mouth at the insect. The insect falls into the water and is quickly devoured.

Page 64

Collective Terms

(A)

1. fir; oak; ash; chestnut;
   Trees
2. shark; salmon; trout; plaice;
   Fish
3. Alps; Rockies; Himalayas; Mourne;
   Mountains
4. Atlantic; Pacific; Indian; Arctic;
   Oceans
5. Japan; Ireland; Greenland; France;
   Countries
6. New York; Moscow; Peking; Dublin;
   Cities
7. canoe; punt; barge; catamaran;
   Boats
8. guitar; flute; violin; mandolin;
   Musical instruments
9. Viper; python; cobra; asp;
   Snakes
10. Pluto; Venus; Mars; Saturn;
    Planets

(C)

1. a **tribe** of goats.
2. a **swarm** of insects.
3. a **brood** of chickens.
4. a **pack** of cards.
5. a **skulk** of foxes.
6. a **swarm** of bees.
7. a **nest** of mice.
8. a **gaggle** of geese.
9. a **bunch** of grapes.
10. a **pride** of lions.
11. a **litter** of pups.
12. a **pack** of wolves.
13. a **school** of whales.
14. a **barren** of mules.
15. a **flight** of swallows.
16. a **team** of horses.

Page 65

An Amazon Tribe

1. Where does Dako live?
   Dako lives in the Amazon jungle.
2. What is the name of his tribe?
   They are called the Xingu tribe.
3. Why does the tribe live near the river?
   They chose this site because of the need for a regular supply of fish and fresh water.
4. How was the hut built?
   First, they cleared the area of forest where they wanted to build. One palm tree was left standing.
   Around this central pole they built a large wooden frame of bamboos. Next, the cone-shaped hut was thatched and lined with palm leaves and sheets of bark.
5. What is the purpose of the fire?
   The fire helps to keep away beetles, flies and mosquitos.
6. How are the Xingus like the Stone Age men?
   They fish in hollowed-out tree trunks.
7. What food do Dako and his friends eat?
   They eat fish, animals, birds, wild berries, honey and bananas.
8. What weapons have the Xingus?
   They hunt with blow-pipes and large spears.
9. How do they catch fish?
   They harpoon them with sharp, pointed spears.
10. How is the poison extracted from the roots of the cassava?
    The roots of the cassava are peeled and soaked in water to remove their poison.

Page 67

Defence and Attack

(A)

1. I goad and puck people with my horns.
   Goat
2. I grip and pinch you with my nippers.
   Crab
3. I swoop and snatch my prey with my talons.
   Eagle
4. I use my sharp teeth and claws to kill.
   Tiger
5. I hiss and frighten people with my forked tongue.
   Snake
6. I attack with my strong ivory tusks.
   Elephant
7. I use my prickly spines to defend myself.
   Hedgehog
8. I float in the sea and sting you.
   Jellyfish
9. I live in jungle swamps and have powerful jaws and tail.
   Crocodile
10. I crush my prey to death with my long, scaly body.
    Boa Constrictor

(B)

1. Cow is to byre as horse is to **stable**.
2. Butterfly is to caterpillar as frog is to **tadpole**.
3. Beef is to cow as mutton is to **sheep**.
4. Hoof is to horse as **paw** is to dog.

Page 67 continued

(C)

1. A vehicle used by the army.
   Jeep
2. A wild plant in the garden.
   Weed
3. An animal with antlers.
   Deer
4. A vegetable like an onion.
   Beet
5. The meat of a cow.
   Beef
6. To shed tears.
   Weep
7. To spy through the keyhole
   Peep
8. Part of your foot.
   Heel
9. Another word for 'humble'.
   Meek
10. Used for winding thread and fishing tackle.
    Reel

Page 68

(E) Like and Unlike

1. Which is an insect?
   Bee
2. Which is a flat fish?
   Plaice
3. Which grows in the garden?
   Flower
4. Which is a wild pig?
   Boar
5. Which is a collection of animals?
   Herd
6. Which is a tree?
   Beech
7. Which is a wild animal?
   Hare
8. Which is a fox's home?
   Lair
9. Which is a female sheep?
   Ewe
10. Which means 'rough'?
    Coarse

(F) 'A' and 'An'

1. Mary saw **an** owl swoop down and kill **a** mouse.
2. **An** eel wriggles like **a** worm.
3. **An** oyster lives in **a** shell.
4. **A** spider is not **an** insect.
5. **A** hyena makes **an** unusual sound.
6. **A** rabbit lives in **an** underground home.
7. **A** flatworm is usually smaller than **an** earthworm.

Page 71

The Queen Bee

1. Where does the queen lay her eggs?
   She lays them in the brood cells in the hive.
2. What are male bees called?
   The males are called drones.
3. What is the importance of 'royal jelly'?
   The queen bee feeds on royal jelly, needed for her to lay eggs successfully.
4. When do bees usually swarm?
   They swarm when the hive becomes overcrowded.
5. Why are there nurse-bees in the hive?
   The nurse-bees look after the larvae.
6. Why is the queen so important for the survival of the hive?
   The queen lays all the eggs, so making possible the continuing survival of the hive.
7. How does the queen display her strength and superiority?
   She tests her drone suitors, flying higher and higher until only the greatest and strongest drone is left.
8. What happens the queen's husband?
   After the wedding flight, the queen's husband dies.
9. What happens when there are two queens in a hive?
   The two queens duel to the death.
10. Describe the queen bee.
    She is bigger and stronger than the workers or other male bees in the hive. She wears a beautiful chocolate-brown dress, striped with bands of gold.

a grain of **sugar**.
a pinch of **salt**.
a morsel of **food**.
a pat of **butter**.
a flake of **snow**.
a speck of **dirt**.
a posy of **flowers**.
a crumb of **bread**.
a splinter of **glass**.
a drop of **water**.

Page 72

Insects

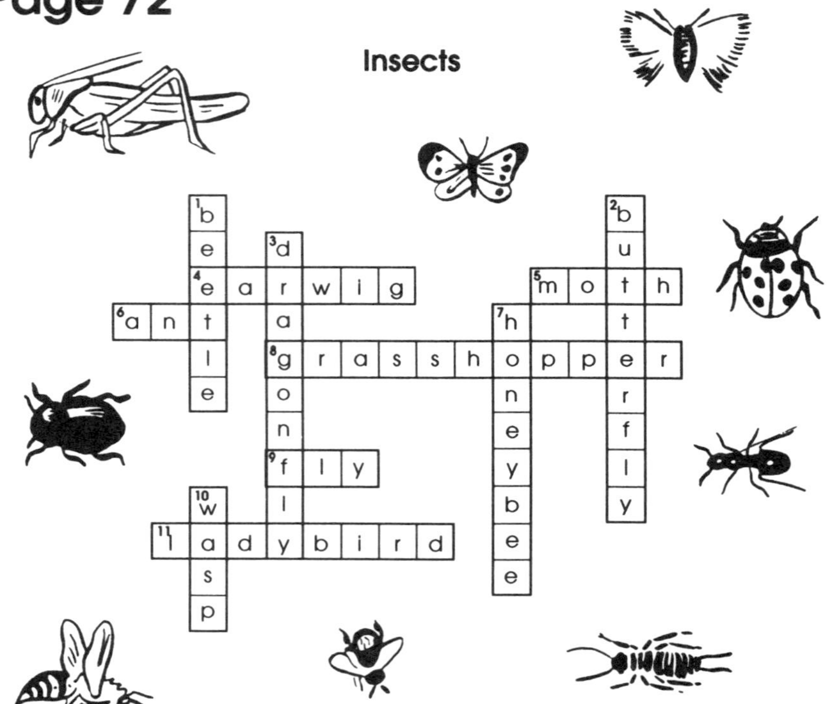

Across
4. Earwig
5. Moth
6. Ant
8. Grasshopper
9. Fly
11. Ladybird

Down
1. Beetle
2. Butterfly
3. Dragonfly
7. Honeybee
10. Wasp

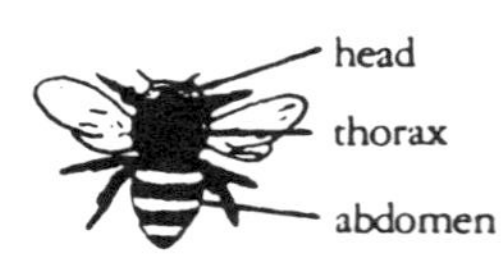

Page 73

More Confusing Words

(A) Did or Done

1. Where **did** they build the hut?
2. Dako's sister **did** not know if the stew was **done** or not.
3. Dana **did** basket weaving while Dako **did** the wood carvings.
4. The work was **done** but the chief **did** not know who had **done** it.
5. **Did** the hunter kill the jaguar? Yes, he **did**.

(B) Of and Off

1. The referee ordered the player **off** the field at the end **of** the game.
2. The tall runner set **off** before the rest **of** the field.
3. The fox ran **off** with two **of** mother's hens.
4. The man took **off** his coat and jumped **off** the rock.
5. Joan, the baby **of** the family, was afraid **of** the big dog next door.
6. Angela turned **off** the television set before going **off** to bed.
7. The two **of** them strolled **off** down the dusty road.
8. At the far end **of** the field the player was carried **off** on a stretcher.
9. Which **of** you tore **off** the new cover **of** my book.
10. He was so well **off** that he gave much **of** his money to charitable organisations.

(C) There and Their

1. The swallows were **there** with **their** friends the house martins.
2. Some birds obtain **their** food by digging with **their** bills.
3. To **their** amazement the penguins fluttered **their** wings and waddled towards **their** camera.
4. The killer whales seized **their** victims in **their** jaws and disappeared.
5. **There** is a kingfisher on that rock over **there**.
6. **There** were hundreds of crows flying home to **their** nests in the woods.
7. The barn swallows built **their** nests **there** last year.
8. Scientists came to **their** village to study **their** habits and customs.

Page 75

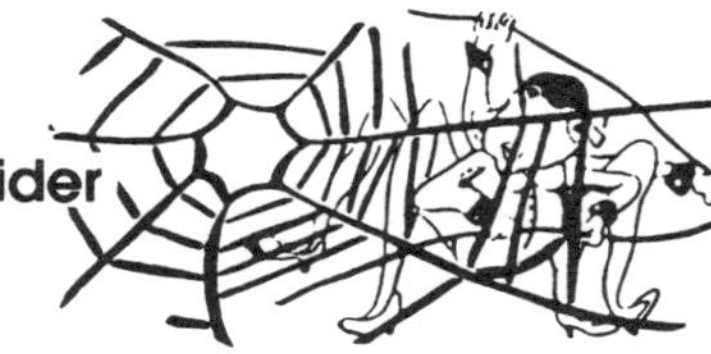

The Garden Spider

1. What is the spider's favourite food?
The spider likes to eat flies and other insects.
2. How does she gather it?
She spins a web to entrap the insects.
3. Why is the garden spider's web sticky?
Some of the threads are coated with sticky beads of glue.
4. How does she avoid being trapped?
Her feet are covered with an oily substance which helps her to glide over the surface of the web.
6. What are 'palps'?
'Palps' are a pair of hooked feelers which the spider uses to eat with.
7. How is she able to travel about quickly?
Her many legs help her to travel quickly.
8. Write the following words in sentences.
palps, spinnerets, claws, gnats.
When the spider eats she uses a pair of hooked feelers called 'palps'.
The spider has six spinning fingers called 'spinnerets'.
She has the most beautiful pointed claws at the tip of each of her eight hairy legs.
She sometimes works throughout the night, weaving and spinning the web into shape, in order to catch the early morning gnats and flies.
9. Describe briefly and clearly how the garden spider's web is made.
10. Where in the garden would you expect to find a spider's web?
Corner of a garden shed, between flowers and bushes.

Pages 78 and 79

1. Which spider can change its colour?
   The crab spider can change its colour.
2. Which spider takes good care of its young?
   The wolf spider takes good care of its young.
3. Which spider often devours its husband?
   The black widow spider often devours its husband.
4. Which spider spins a cobweb?
   The house spider spins a cobweb.
5. Which spider creeps up silently on its victim?
   The zebra spider creeps up silently on its victim.
6. Which spider dies after laying its eggs.
   The garden spider dies after laying its eggs.

Page 79

Homonyms

1.	Seven days	**(week)**
	Feeble	**(weak)**
2.	Sixty minutes	**(hour)**
	Belonging to us	**(our)**
3.	Expensive	**(dear)**
	An animal	**(deer)**
4.	Shines in sky	**(sun)**
	A male child	**(son)**
5.	Quietness	**(peace)**
	A part	**(piece)**
6.	To pull	**(tow)**
	Of the foot	**(toe)**
7.	Of a ship	**(sail)**
	To sell	**(sale)**
8.	A story	**(tale)**
	Part of a dog	**(tail)**
9.	Useless	**(waste)**
	Part of the body	**(waist)**
10.	A strand	**(beach)**
	Type of tree	**(beech)**
11.	An animal	**(hare)**
	Of the head	**(hair)**

Page 79 continued

12.	Verb 'to hear'	**(heard)**
	A group of animals	**(herd)**
13.	Verb 'to know'	**(knew)**
	Not used before	**(new)**
14.	To use a needle	**(sew)**
	To place seeds	**(sow)**
15.	Of glass	**(pane)**
	Ache	**(pain)**
16.	For a lock	**(key)**
	A dock	**(quay)**

(B)

1. It was **eight** o'clock before I **ate** a morsel of food.
2. He hid the **whole** amount of his savings in a deep **hole**.
3. When you **bury** that red **berry** it will grow into a tree.
4. It was an **hour** later that **our** boat departed from the quay.
5. Everyone **knew** that he bought a **new** bicycle.
6. She **read** the title on the cover of the **red** book.
7. The trainer **knows** that the player's **nose** is fractured.
8. The ram and the **ewe** stood near the **yew** tree.
9. Harry **would** like to go for a nature walk through the **wood**.
10. She **threw** the ball **through** the window.
11. He was **quite** right. The place was very **quiet**.
12. Which **one** of you **won** the race?
13. The **fair** haired man thought the **fare** on the bus was very dear.

(C)

1. Which is a fireplace?
   grate
2. Which is a group of people?
   team
3. Which is a fruit?
   pear
4. Which is a vegetable?
   leek
5. Which is a branch?
   bough

Page 80

Words and Nature

(A)

1. The **bee** hums.
2. The **lamb** bleats.
3. The **horse** neighs.
4. The **donkey** brays.
5. The **dog** barks.
6. The **lion** roars.
7. The **monkey** chatters.
8. The **bear** growls.
9. The **gorilla** gibbers.
10. The **cat** purrs.
11. The **cow** lows.
12. The **bull** bellows.
13. The **duck** quacks.
14. The **hen** cackles.
15. The **mouse** squeaks.
16. The **frog** croaks.
17. The **swan** whistles.
18. The **rabbit** squeals.
19. The **pigeon** coos.
20. The **sparrow** chirps.

(B)

1. I awoke the **next** day as fresh as a **daisy**.
2. The table he **made** was as sturdy as an **oak**.
3. He **won** the race because he ran as fast as a **hare**.
4. Her hair was as black as **coal** and her skin was as white as **snow**.
5. The gymnast on the **mat** was as agile as a **monkey**.
6. I will be as busy as a **bee** for the rest of the **day**.
7. After winning the **race** she was as **happy** as a lark.
8. The old man of the **tribe** was as wise as an **owl**.
9. Anyone who **thinks** the Earth is flat is as mad as a **March hare**.
10. If you keep eating all that **food** you will be as fat as a **pig**.

Page 82

The Mute Swan

1. Where do you usually see mute swans?
   They live all year round on our rivers, lakes and ponds.
2. What use does she make of her webbed feet?
   Her broad webbed feet help her to glide gracefully along our waterways.
3. How does she find her food?
   She grazes on weeds and grasses to be found just below the water surface. She enjoys a tasty meal of eel grass and water insects at the water's edge.
4. Is the swan a good flier?
   The swan is a powerful flier, and can cruise along at speeds of 60-80 kilometres an hour.
5. What special name has each parent?
   The female swan is called a pen and the male swan is called a cob.
6. What materials do the parents use to build their nest?
   They use a combination of reeds, weeds and grasses.
7. Why does the swan dry her feathers before sitting on the eggs?
   She dries her feathers in order to keep the eggs warm.
8. What enemies has the swan?
   The thieving rats and hungry otters are her enemies.
9. What are young swans called?
   Young swans are called cygnets.
10. How do they go sightseeing?
    They go sightseeing by travelling on their parents' backs.
11. When do cygnets become adult swans?
    It takes about three years for cygnets to mature into adult swans.

Page 84

Quotation Marks

(A)

1. Paul has ruined my painting sobbed Lorraine.
   “Paul has ruined my painting,” sobbed Lorraine.
2. Did you hear about the flood in Main Street asked Neil.
   “Did you hear about the flood in Main Street?” asked Neil.
3. I sentence you to one month in prison said the judge.
   “I sentence you to one month in prison,” said the judge.
4. Once upon a time there was a small cottage in the woods whispered the storyteller.
   “Once upon a time there was a small cottage in the woods,” whispered the storyteller.
5. The huntsman roared The fox is making for the woods.
   The huntsman roared, “The fox is making for the woods.”
6. Kevin promised I will return your books on Friday.
   Kevin promised, “I will return your books on Friday.”
7. Nora wished I hope granny brings one of her chocolate cakes.
   Nora wished, “I hope granny brings one of her chocolate cakes.”
8. I know nothing about the stolen watch lied Conor.
   “I know nothing about the stolen watch,” lied Conor.
9. Do not stray from the forest path warned Little Red Riding Hood’s grandmother.
   “Do not stray from the forest path,” warned Little Red Riding Hood’s grandmother.
10. The captain urged We must try harder in the second half.
    The captain urged, “We must try harder in the second half.”

Page 84 continued

(B)

yesterday pedro and isabella had great fun in the orange grove the day was sunny and warm and suitable for orange picking isabella enjoyed picking the fruit she wore gloves to save the skin of the oranges being spoilt her brother pedro climbed the ladder and picked oranges from the top of the tree just imagine isabella said pedro this orange I'm picking may be eaten by an irish boy at noon their father arrived in a truck to collect the fruit he was very pleased with their work they quickly loaded the fruit onto the truck their father allowed them to travel with him to the market in madrid as they sped along the dusty road towards the big city he turned to them and said next sunday i will bring the pair of you to see the great carlos fight the bulls in valencia.

Yesterday Pedro and Isabella had great fun in the orange grove. The day was sunny and warm and suitable for orange picking. Isabella enjoyed picking the fruit. She wore gloves to save the skin of the oranges being spoilt. Her brother Pedro climbed the ladder and picked oranges from the top of the tree. “Just imagine Isabella,” said Pedro, “this orange I'm picking may be eaten by an Irish boy.” At noon their father arrived in a truck to collect the fruit. He was very pleased with their work. They quickly loaded the fruit onto the truck. Their father allowed them to travel with him to the market in Madrid. As they sped along the dusty road towards the big city, he turned to them and said, “Next Sunday I will bring the pair of you to see the Great Carlos fight the bulls in Valencia.”

Page 86

Creatures of the Night

1. What is a mammal?
   Mammals are warm-blooded animals and their babies are born alive, not hatched from an egg.
2. What do bats like to eat?
   Bats like to eat beetles, moths and spiders. Some bats like fruit, especially bananas.
3. How do they navigate in pitch darkness?
   The bat sends out loud squeaks. The sound bounces off surrounding objects and the echo is picked up by the bat's keen sense of hearing. In this way it avoids crashing into objects.
4. How do bats capture their food?
   They trap insects in their mouth or wings.
5. What is peculiar about the horseshoe bat?
   It has a very funny snout and squeaks through its nostrils.
6. Where would you expect to find a colony of bats?
   You would expect to find them in an old castle, cave, mine shaft or empty dwelling.
7. Why does a bat hang upside down?
   They do this for their own safety. If they are disturbed or alarmed during the night they simply drop into the air and fly away.
8. Describe the pipistrelle.
   The pipistrelle has a tiny body like that of a mouse. Its thin silky wings are joined to the rest of its body by a web of silk.

Page 87

Adverbs

(A)

1. He *quick* swam the first length of the pool.
   He **quickly** swam the first length of the pool.
2. She argued *bitter* with her mother.
   She argued **bitterly** with her mother.
3. The sun shone *brilliant* over the crowded stadium.
   The sun shone **brilliantly** over the crowded stadium.
4. The actress spoke *calm* and *slow*.
   The actress spoke **calmly** and **slowly**.
5. He won *superb*.
   He won **superbly**.
6. She *brave* rescued the drowning puppy.
   She **bravely** rescued the drowning puppy.
7. The captain spoke *quiet* to his team.
   The captain spoke **quietly** to his team.
8. The garda (police officer) eyed the man *suspicious*.
   The garda (police officer) eyed the man **suspiciously**.
9. We sat *patient* in the waiting room.
   We sat **patiently** in the waiting room.
10. The king ruled his kingdom *wise*.
    The king ruled his kingdom **wisely**.

Page 87 continued

(B)

1. The bored child yawned *lazy*.
   The bored child yawned **lazily**.
2. The footballer fell *heavy* on his shoulder.
   The footballer fell **heavily** on his shoulder.
3. The bee works *busy* from dawn to dusk.
   The bee works **busily** from dawn to dusk.
4. The train rumbled *noisy* towards the city.
   The train rumbled **noisily** towards the city.
5. The baby gurgled *happy* in the cot.
   The baby gurgled **happily** in the cot.
6. Santa Claus chuckled *merry* to himself.
   Santa Claus chuckled **merrily** to himself.
7. We returned to the haunted castle and entered *wary*.
   We returned to the haunted castle and entered **warily**.
8. The bull looked *angry* at the matador.
   The bull looked **angrily** at the matador.
9. The level of the water rose *steady*.
   The level of the water rose **steadily**.
10. The impatient businessman left *hasty*.
    The impatient businessman left **hastily**.

Page 89

The Swallow

1. Describe how the swallow builds its nest.
   It is made of moist mud, soft grasses and straw cemented together into a mud-like saucer. They find the mud in a nearby pool or brook and use their wide bills to scoop it up.

2. How does the swallow catch flies and gnats?
   They catch flies and gnats on the wing. Swallows fly along with their beaks open, skimming the air for insects.

3. Why do swallows fly to Africa?
   They go to Africa for the warmth and the abundance of food, both of which are scarce in Britain during the winter months.

4. Can you explain what 'migration' means?
   Migration is the routine journey of a species of bird to another area for a period of the year in order. This is to avoid extreme changes of living conditions which can result from seasonal variations.

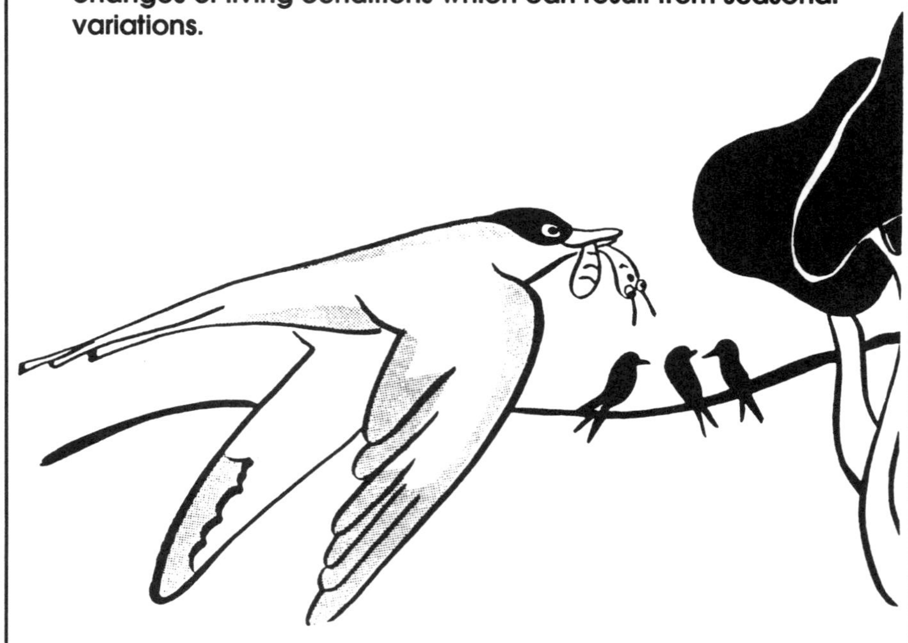

Name: ____________________ Date: ____________________

Nouns

Nouns are naming words.

Write ten nouns that you can see in the picture.

1. ____________________
2. ____________________
3. ____________________
4. ____________________
5. ____________________
6. ____________________
7. ____________________
8. ____________________
9. ____________________
10. ____________________

NOW

- Write lists of nouns under the following headings:

Cities	Jobs	Your own choice

Name: ______________________________ Date: ______________________________

Adjectives

Adjectives are describing words. They describe nouns.

Underline all the adjectives in this passage.

In the autumn the female garden spider builds a soft cradle of smooth silk for her small family. It is shaped like a small blackbird's egg. She lays hundreds of tiny eggs inside the silken cocoon. This is hidden among the overhanging leaves or gloomy crevices under the window ledges and doors.

Choose the correct adjective from the box to fill in the blank spaces in the story.

- feathered
- happy
- old
- tiny
- touching
- black
- main
- pretty
- dry
- hungry

Mrs Jones was an __________ lady. She lived in a __________ cottage on the __________ street of our __________ village. Every day she would feed the __________ birds with pieces of __________ bread. The __________ birds would fight off the sparrows to eat the bread. It was a __________ sight to see this __________ woman with all her __________ friends.

Name: ______________________ Date: ______________________

Verbs

Complete this table.

Present tense Today I ...	Past tense Yesterday I ...	Past participle I have ...
am	was	
beat		
begin		begun
blow		
build		
buy		
choose		
come	came	
creep	crept	
do		
draw		
drive		
eat		eaten
fall		
fly		flown
forget		
give	gave	
go		
grow		
hide		hidden
know		
ring	rang	
rise		
shake		
speak		
stand	stood	
steal		
swim		swum
take		
write	wrote	

Name: ______________________ Date: ______________________

Sentences

Sentences start with a capital letter and end with a full stop. They must make sense.

Write ten sentences about a visit to an airport.

Helpful words and ideas

... with my best friend ... a tour of ... motorway ... big car park ... large, modern building ... hundreds of passengers ... hustle and bustle ... tickets ... suitcases ... saying goodbye ... busy workers ... jumbo jets ... roar of the planes ... taking off ... landing.

Name: ______________________ Date: ______________________

Punctuation of speech

These ten sentences need full stops, commas, quotation marks and apostrophes.

1. Please dont play with that air gun asked my father

____

2. It isnt loaded I answered

____

3. Dont argue dad replied

____

4. But it cant do any harm I insisted

____

5. Youre very obstinate sighed dad

____

6. Ive got the safety catch on I explained

____

7. Im sorry I ever bought it dad declared

____

8. Thats because I like to load it with pellets I answered

____

9. Theres going to be an accident one day dad grumbled

____

10. Im perfectly capable of handling a loaded air gun I said as I tripped over the mat

____

- Punctuate this more difficult passage. Underline all the speech first to help you decide where to put the quotation marks.

little johnny was emptying his pockets before going to bed

Where did you get this money from his mother asked

fred gave it to me for doing him a favour answered johnny

what exactly did you do for him his mother said

well said johnny i was bashing him on the head with a stick and he asked me to stop

Name: ______________________ Date: ______________________

Plurals 1

Write examples to prove the rules.

RULE	EXAMPLES	
Most nouns simply add -s to the singular.	1. 2. 3. 4. 5.	6. 7. 8. 9. 10.
Most nouns ending in -s, -x, -sh, -ch, -ss form their plural by adding -es to the singular.	1. 2. 3. 4. 5.	6. 7. 8. 9. 10.
Nouns ending in -f or -fe in general change the -f or -fe for -v and add -es.	1. 2. 3. 4. 5.	
Nouns ending in -y with a consonant before, change the -y to -i and add -es. If there is a vowel before the -y, add -s.	1. 2. 3. 4. 5.	6. 7. 8. 9. 10.

35 marks

NOW

- Write some sentences using the words you have chosen.

1. ______________________
2. ______________________
3. ______________________
4. ______________________
5. ______________________

Name: ______________________ Date: ______________________

Plurals 2

Write examples to prove the rules.

RULE	EXAMPLES
A small number of nouns remain unchanged in the singular and plural.	
Some nouns ending in -o add -es in the plural. Others add -s.	
Some nouns have no singular.	
A few nouns form their plurals by changing their middle letters.	

- Write some sentences using the words you have chosen.

____

____

____

____

____

Name: ____________________ Date: ____________________

Letter box

1	2	3
4	5	6
7	8	9
10	11	12

The letter box hides a secret letter.

- Identify the sentences which have direct speech.
- Colour the squares which have the same numbers as the direct speech sentences.
- What letter is revealed?
- Add speech marks around the direct speech.

1 Where's the spinach? asked Popeye.

2 Dinosaur steak again! moaned Fred Flintstone.

3 What big ears you've got Mr Spock said Red Riding Hood.

4 Dorothy complained that her red shoes were killing her.

5 Sorry can't stay, must fly called Superman.

6 Robin reminded Batman that he was wearing his underpants outside his trousers.

7 Dr Doolittle wondered when the animals would reply.

8 Tarzan, I'm sick and tired of doing the ironing grumbled Jane.

9 The dentist rang Dracula to tell him his false teeth were ready.

10 You can come out now Rambo, the mouse has gone called his mother.

11 Indiana Jones, what a strange name, wouldn't Smith be better? asked the teacher.

12 The garage informed Dr Frankenstein that the bodywork was finished.

Name: ______________________________ Date: ______________________________

Opposites

Match the opposites.

question	shallow
open	poverty
correct	rude
arrive	depart
success	junior
senior	difficult
innocent	wrong
sweet	import
tame	wild
polite	interior
quiet	answer
giant	scarce
plentiful	guilty
exterior	barren
wealth	closed
export	stale
private	noisy
easy	failure
deep	public
fertile	sour
fresh	dwarf

Name: ______________________ Date: ______________________

Dictionary work

It is important that you know the alphabet before you can use your dictionary.

A B C D E F G H I J K L M N O P Q R S T U V W X Y Z

Answer these puzzles. Put the answers in alphabetical order.

	Answer	Alphabetical order
1. A female sheep.		
2. You see with them.		
3. A letter that you drink.		
4. A line of people waiting for something.		
5. A letter that is a vegetable.		
6. Ships sail on it. It rhymes with tea.		
7. Frozen water.		
8. Half of 160.		
9. Containing nothing.		
10. Grapes grow on it.		

WORDS OF INTEREST

Look at the letters which make up these words. What makes these words special? You should look up the meanings of the words in your dictionary.

BOOKKEEPER ______________________

INDIVISIBILITY ______________________

STRENGTH ______________________

FACETIOUS ______________________

QUEUE ______________________

Name: ______________________ Date: ______________________

Letters

Write a thankyou letter.

A VERY SPECIAL THANK YOU

- When you have finished go back and check your work.
- Is the address in the right place and is it correctly punctuated?
- Have you started and ended the letter in an appropriate way?
- Is the letter set out in paragraphs?

Name: ______________________ Date: ______________________

Vocabulary

Special words exist to describe 'a lot of' the following. Use your dictionary to find what they are.

a lot of ships	fl ____________
a lot of cattle	h ____________
a lot of money	f ____________
a lot of riotous people	m ____________
a lot of snow in a storm	b ____________

There are often special words to describe large sizes. Use your dictionary to find out what they are.

a big ship	l ____________
a big man	g ____________
a big pond	l ____________
a big tent	m ____________
a big stone	b ____________

'Get' is a word we tend to overuse. There is usually a better word. Use your dictionary to find some alternatives.

to get smaller	d ____________
to get better	i ____________
to get better from an illness	r ____________
to get going	b ____________
to get on a horse	m ____________

'Nice' is also an overused word. Use your dictionary to find alternatives.

a nice jacket (up to date, the latest design)	fa ____________
a nice meal (tasty, satisfying)	ap ____________
a nice book (gripping, very interesting)	fa ____________
a nice surprise (giving happiness)	pl ____________
a nice conversation (topics appeal to you)	in ____________

Name: ______________________ Date: ______________________

Chats

"These are speech marks"

- *When people speak we put the words they say inside speech marks, like this: "How are you?"*
- *When you are writing speech you let the reader know who is speaking by adding words like said, shouted and called.*
- *Write out the story, putting the words in bubbles into speech marks. The first one has been done for you.*

"I'm hungry," said Zoe.

- Make up another chat between Claire and Zoe.

Name: ____________________ Date: ____________________

Be a proofreader

- Proofreaders use special marks to point out mistakes.
- These paragraphs tell a story, but there are some mistakes.
- Use the proofreader's marks to correct them.

I have always wanted my own dog, you can keep posh bicks and comupters, all I want is a litel furry friend. I want a yorkshire Terrier.

My dog says dogs are nasti smelly yappi fings that are alwise under yor fet and make messes in the garden he says I will hav to weight until I have a home of my own, then I can do as I like. Sometimes I relly hate him.

Two weeks before my birthday I got home from shool. I was wet, again, it always rans wen school finishes. Mum was siting in the kitchen drinking coffe with her friend, she cald out Helo and told me to put my wet stuff on the boiler to dry, I walked thru the kitchen and saw ...

Proofreader's marks

- Make a capital letter
- Make a small letter
- Add a full stop
- Add a comma
- Wrong spelling
- Move something
- New paragraph

NOW

- Write out the correct version and finish the story.